Learn Science with Mo

PLANTS

Paul Mason

Michael Buxton

Published in 2025 by Enslow Publishing, LLC
2544 Clinton Street
Buffalo, NY 14224

First published in Great Britain in 2024 by Wayland

Copyright © Hodder & Stoughton Limited, 2024

Editor: John Hort
Design: Collaborate
Illustrations: Michael Buxton
Science consultant: Peter Riley

All rights reserved. No part of this book may be reproduced in any form without permission in writing from the publisher, except by a reviewer.

Manufactured in the United States of America

CPSIA compliance information: Batch #CSENS25: For further information contact Enslow Publishing LLC, New York, New York at 1-800-398-2504.

Please visit our website, www.enslowpublishing.com. For a free color catalog of all our high-quality books, call toll free 1-800-398-2504 or fax 1-877-980-4454.

Cataloging-in-Publication Data

Names: Mason, Paul, author. | Buxton, Michael, illustrator.
Title: Plants / by Paul Mason, illustrated by Michael Buxton.
Description: Buffalo, NY : Enslow Publishing, 2025. |
Series: Learn science with Mo | Includes glossary.
Identifiers: ISBN 9781978538832 (pbk.) | ISBN 9781978538849 (library bound) |
ISBN 9781978538856 (ebook)
Subjects: LCSH: Plants--Juvenile literature. | Botany--Juvenile literature.
Classification: LCC QK49.M376 2025 | DDC 580--dc23

Find us on

Contents

Crash! Mo feels bad	4
All kinds of plants	6
Watering duty	8
Rain and sunshine	10
Leaves	12
Deciduous and evergreen	14
Flowers	16
Bees and insects	18
Fruit and seeds	20
Growing seeds	22
Seedling separation	24
Feeding the trees	26
Plants and the planet	28
Glossary	30
Books to read/Places to visit	31
Answers	32

The words in **bold** are in the glossary on page 30.

Mo, Millie, and Dizzy are playing softball. Mo gets a great hit on the ball – but it does not turn out well.

Oh, no!

Why not go and offer to help the owner this weekend, Mo? It would be a nice way to make up for breaking the greenhouse.

Great idea!

CONNIE FERN'S PLANTS AND TREES

Nursery and gardening services

The greenhouse is owned by Connie Fern. It is part of her nursery, where she grows plants to sell.

I THOUGHT NURSERIES WERE FOR BABIES?

This one must be for baby plants.

PLANTS FOR SALE

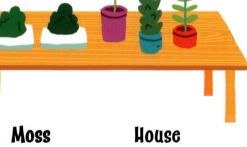

Moss **House plants** **Shrubs** **Flowering plants** **Trees**

Connie tells Mo and his friends that she grows all kinds of plants. She would love to have them help her.

I have a secret plan – to teach these little monsters how amazing plants are. Maybe they will decide to become gardeners, like me!

All kinds of PLANTS

On Saturday morning, the friends arrive at the nursery to start helping Connie Fern.

Connie explains to Mo what the two main kinds of plants are at the nursery. Mo tells his friends.

THE FIRST KIND ARE FLOWERING PLANTS. THE FLOWERS ARE PART OF HOW THE PLANTS **REPRODUCE**.

Forget-me-nots **Sunflower** **Tree**

Most people know flowering plants like these forget-me-nots ... or this sunflower. But lots of trees have flowers, too.

NOT ALL PLANTS MAKE FLOWERS.

Moss **Fern** **Fir tree**

These little mosses, the giant fern, and trees that make **cones**, like fir trees, do not flower. They're still pretty, though!

All plants have one thing in common. They can make their own food in a process called **photosynthesis.**

> WHAT? HOW IS THAT POSSIBLE?

You will discover more about photosynthesis when we look at leaves, on pages 12-13. Did you know that plants make YOUR food, too? Whatever you eat, if you trace it backward the food originally came from plants. It's the same for other animals, too.

Grass   Rabbit eats grass   Fox eats rabbit

Algae   Parrotfish eats algae   Reef shark eats parrotfish

> SO, WITHOUT PLANTS ANIMALS COULD NOT LIVE?

That is correct, Mo. Plants help life on Earth survive in other ways, too — you can find out about those on pages 28–29.

WATERING duty

Connie Fern explains that to make their own food, one of the things plants need is water. Mo's first job is watering duty.

WHICH PART SHOULD I WATER?

Water the **soil**, Mo. Water gets into a plant by its roots, then travels to the other parts. The roots grow underground:

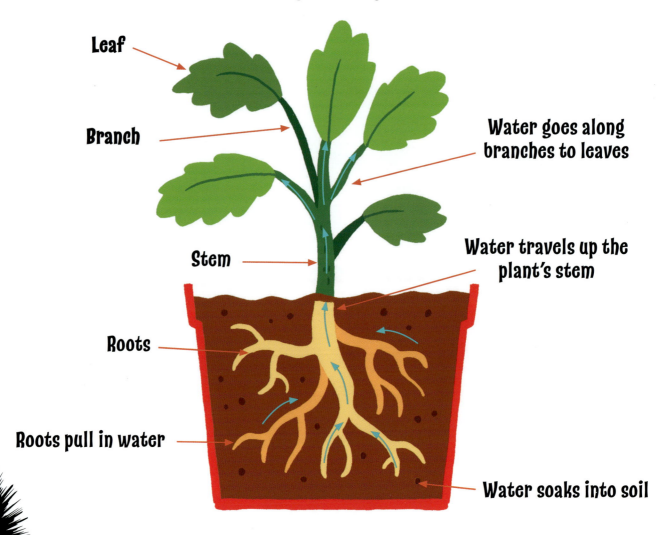

- Leaf
- Branch
- Stem
- Roots
- Roots pull in water
- Water goes along branches to leaves
- Water travels up the plant's stem
- Water soaks into soil

Roots have other jobs, too. See if you, Millie, and Dizzy can figure out which of these jobs roots might do, Mo!

A. Hold the plant in place.

If plants didn't have roots they might blow away. Yes!

B. Help plants talk to each other.

No, plants can't talk!

C. Get nutrients (things the plant needs to help it grow) from the soil.

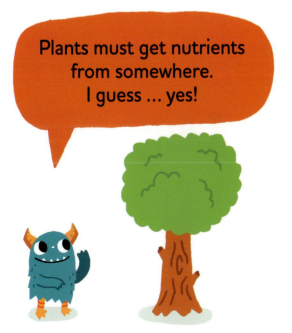

Plants must get nutrients from somewhere. I guess … yes!

D. Store food for the plant.

Well, root vegetables like carrots are food, so … yes!

Did Mo and the others answer correctly? Find out if they were right on page 32.

RAIN AND SUNSHINE

Mo and the others go outside to water some plants that are growing in pots. Suddenly, though, heavy rain starts to fall.

Fortunately, the sun soon comes out. The friends dry off quickly.

Everything dries out because of **evaporation.**
The heat from the sun has turned the water into a **gas** called water vapor.

A kind of evaporation called transpiration happens in the leaves of plants:

Usually, we cannot see transpiration. But Mo, there IS an experiment that will show it to you.

OK! I LIKE EXPERIMENTS.

Wrap a leafy plant in a clear plastic bag and tape it closed.

Leave it in the sunlight for an hour.

What do you notice, Mo?

IT'S ALL CLOUDY AND WET INSIDE!

Exactly. The water came from the leaves as water vapor. When it touched the plastic bag, it changed back to water.

Transpiration pulls water up from the plant's roots, like someone sucking on a straw.

LEAVES

Mo and Dizzy soon get their next job. Connie wants them to take some plants sunbathing!

DO THEY WANT TO GET A TAN?

No, Mo – the plants are going outside for a meal. Plants with green leaves use light to make a food called glucose. They do this using photosynthesis.

Photosynthesis uses light, water, and a gas called **carbon dioxide**:

1. The leaves absorb light energy. They also pull in carbon dioxide from the air.

2. The plants use this energy to change water and carbon dioxide into glucose and oxygen gas.

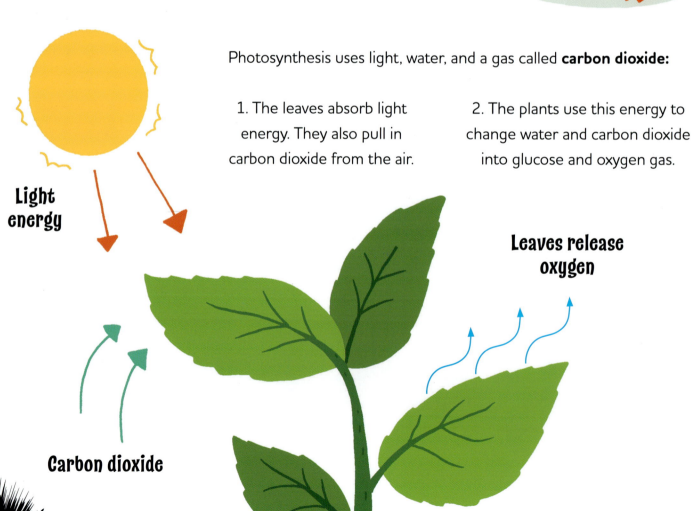

Light energy

Leaves release oxygen

Carbon dioxide

DECIDUOUS and EVERGREEN

Mo's next job is sweeping up fallen leaves from underneath some of Connie's trees.

I LOVE BONFIRES!

Connie wants to make a bonfire using the leaves Mo collects.

Mo, we can make a great bonfire as long as we get the right kinds of leaves. Where could we get them?

HONESTLY? NO IDEA.

No problem — we can find out. We have a choice between leaves from the two main kinds of tree: deciduous and evergreen.

Deciduous tree

Wide, flat leaves

Leaves dry out and fall before the start of winter

Evergreen tree

Thin, needlelike leaves

An evergreen tree's leaves can last up to two years, and can fall out at any time.

Many evergreens grow cones

That's right, Mo. We need wide, flat, dry leaves for a bonfire.
The leaves from a deciduous tree will be best.

FLOWERS

Connie's nursery has lots of nice flowers. Mo is sniffing them to chase away the smell of the bonfire!

ACTUALLY, I'VE NEVER REALLY LOOKED AT A FLOWER BEFORE ...

Look a bit closer, Mo, and you'll see the different parts of a flower.

SNIFF! SNIFF!

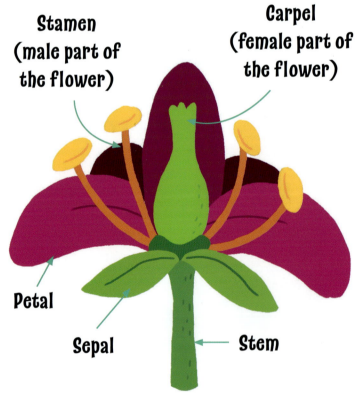

Stamen (male part of the flower)

Carpel (female part of the flower)

Petal

Sepal

Stem

HOW CAN FLOWERS BE MALE AND FEMALE?

To understand that, you will need to find out about something called **pollination**. Bees are going to teach you about pollination on pages 18-19.

Now, though, there is a bit more to find out about the different parts of a flower. The stamen and carpel each have more than one part:

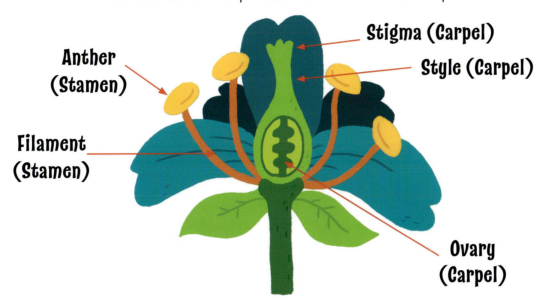

Have a look at these different flowers, Mo, and see if they all have the same parts:

That is correct. Flowers do not all look the same, but they do have the same parts.

Mo is running away from a bee!

BEES AND INSECTS

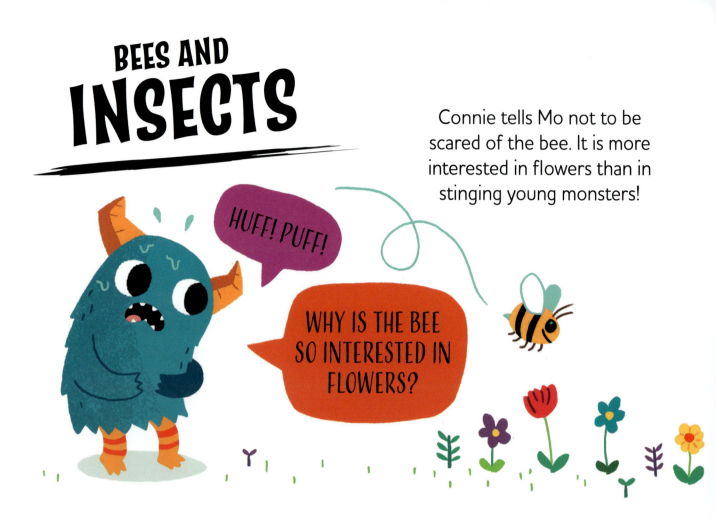

Connie tells Mo not to be scared of the bee. It is more interested in flowers than in stinging young monsters!

The flowers' job is to attract bees and other insects. The insects will help the plants to reproduce. This process is called pollination. It works like this:

1. The bright colors and smell of the flower attract insects. They are looking for **nectar** (as well as pollen to eat).

2. The insect sucks up nectar from the middle of the flower.

As it does this, pollen falls from the male part of the flower into the bee's fuzzy hair.

3. When the insect visits another flower, some of the pollen falls off. It lands in the female part of the flower.

4. The female part of the flower begins to change. It turns into seeds, or fruit.

Pollinators

Bees are the most important pollinators, but they are not the only creatures that help with pollination. Flies, moths, and some other small animals all drink nectar and spread pollen from flower to flower.

FRUIT AND SEEDS

The friends' next job is going to be working with seeds. Connie Fern tells them that fruits and seeds contain everything needed for a new plant to grow.

Connie, can you explain to Mo, Millie, and Dizzy about fruit and seeds?

I'd love to! Let's look at some fruit. Like all fruit, apples come from flowering plants.

Fruit

This is the flesh of the fruit.

The stalk was once the stem, attaching the flower to the plant.

The core grew from the female part of the flower. Part of this became the seed or "pip."

Animals eat the flesh and seeds. They poop the seeds out later and new plants grow in a new place.

Seeds can spread in other ways, too. Some blow away in the wind, or stick to animal fur and are carried off.

No one eats the dusty part at the bottom! It is the dried-out remains of sepals, stamen, stigma, and styles (remind yourself about those on page 17).

Seeds

The seed is the most important part.
This is what a new apple tree could one day grow from.

Inside the seed is the cotyledon, a store of food the seed uses to grow.

The outside is a hard layer.

The parts at the pointy end will grow into the roots and stem. They are too tiny to see with your eyes.

SO IF I SWALLOW APPLE SEEDS ... WILL APPLE TREES GROW IN MY TUMMY?

No, Mo – you will just poop them out a day or two later!

GROWING SEEDS

After telling them about seeds, Connie takes Mo and Millie to the cool storeroom. All kinds of seeds are kept here.

DIZZY DIDN'T WANT TO COME IN. DIZZY'S A CROCODILE AND THEY DON'T LIKE THE COLD.

Seeds do not really like extreme temperature either, Mo. If it is too cold, they will not start to grow, or **germinate**. That is why Connie keeps her seeds in a cool room until she's ready to plant them.

Not all seeds germinate at the same temperature. For example:

Spinach germinates after the soil has been at least 55°F (13°C) for five days.

Eggplants need the soil to be at least 80°F (27°C) for six days.

Mo and Millie's job is to plant one seed in each quarter of the little pot — four seeds in total.

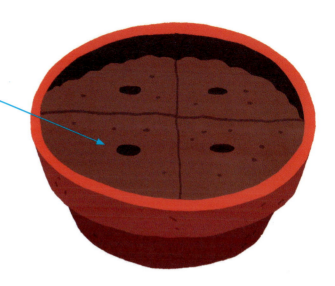

Mo, why do you think the seeds need to go in the middle of each quarter?

I BET IT'S LIKE WHEN ME AND COUSIN RORY DO EXERCISE. WE NEED SPACE!

Correct! Once the seeds start to grow roots, they will need space to spread out.

Next, the pots are moved to a warmer place and watered. Warmth and water will help them germinate.

Seedling SEPARATION

From the seed store, Connie Fern takes the friends to see some baby plants, called seedlings. Dizzy comes, too! Connie explains that the seedlings have grown too big for their pots. Each one has to be given a bigger pot. This will give their roots space to grow.

A plant with more roots can get more water from the soil to help the plant make food.

WHY DO THE ROOTS NEED TO BE BIGGER?

Plants with more roots can grow bigger and faster.

MORE WATER = MORE FOOD = MORE GROWTH

Connie gives each friend their own job:

"I'M PICKING THE SEEDLINGS OUT OF THEIR SMALL CONTAINERS. IT'S NOT THAT EASY WITH MONSTER PAWS!"

"I'm adding some soil to a bigger pot and putting the seedling into it."

"My job is adding labels to the pots so that Connie Fern knows what plants they are."

Let's see if you can remember what Connie has told the monsters about roots:

1. Do roots help plants get:
   a) water
   or
   b) sunlight?

2 Water is one of the things plants need for:
   a) making food
   or
   b) reproducing?

You can find out if you were correct on page 32.

FEEDING THE TREES

Before they finish helping Connie Fern, the friends have one more job to do. They have to feed some trees.

WAIT, WHAT? I THOUGHT PLANTS MADE THEIR OWN FOOD?

Yes, Mo, they do. But as well as water, light, and carbon dioxide, plants need nutrients to grow. These are the most important ones:

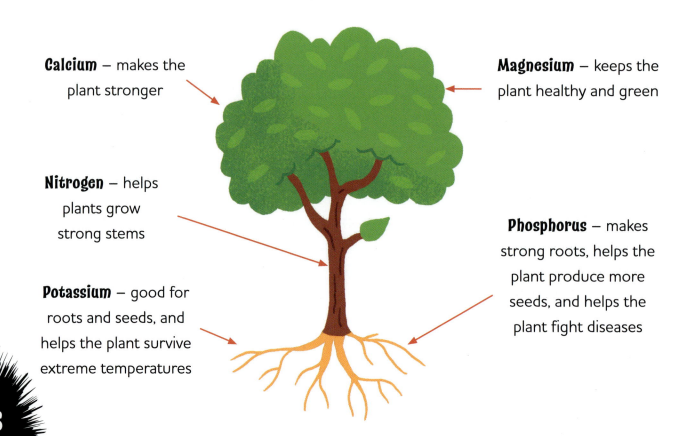

Calcium – makes the plant stronger

Nitrogen – helps plants grow strong stems

Potassium – good for roots and seeds, and helps the plant survive extreme temperatures

Magnesium – keeps the plant healthy and green

Phosphorus – makes strong roots, helps the plant produce more seeds, and helps the plant fight diseases

Most plants get their nutrients from soil. But trees (or any plants) in a pot soon use up the soil's nutrients. More have to be added.

Mo, since Dizzy watered your feet, imagine you're a plant. Which nutrients would you need for:

Healthy roots?   **Growing strong and tall?**   **Having a healthy green color?**

All perfect answers, Mo — well done!

PLANTS and the PLANET

Mo, working with Connie Fern has taught you lots about plants. Here is one more fact: without plants, life on Earth would quickly die out.

Plants save the world, part 1:

Plants provide us with food. Even when we eat meat or fish, the energy it contains originally came from plants.

HUH?

I NEED TO TELL COUSIN RORY ABOUT THIS ...

Plants save the world, part 2:

Plants provide the air we breathe. They take in carbon dioxide and release oxygen. All animals need oxygen to survive.

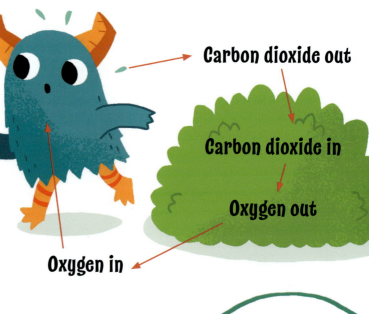

Carbon dioxide out

Carbon dioxide in

Oxygen out

Oxygen in

Plants save the world, part 3:

Plants store carbon in their **structures**. If carbon stayed in the air, it would add to the **greenhouse gases** around our planet. These gases keep in heat.

28

Global warming

Too much heat is now being trapped by greenhouse gases and Earth's temperature is slowly rising. This is called global warming, and it is having terrible effects:

Droughts become more common. Deserts, where few plants grow, spread.

Fierce storms happen more often. Storms flood land with seawater and kill the plants there.

Sea levels are rising, flooding low-lying lands.

The habitats that plants and animals live in change. This makes it hard (or even impossible) for them to survive.

WOW! PLANTS ARE EVEN MORE IMPORTANT THAN I THOUGHT.

Glossary

algae
a type of plant that usually grows in water. Seaweed is a kind of algae, but most algae are much smaller.

branch
the part of a tree that grows away from the middle

carbon dioxide
a gas that makes up about 0.03 percent of air. Although this is a small amount, carbon dioxide causes about 20 percent of global warming.

cone
on a plant, cones are seed containers. They are circular at the bottom and narrower at the top. When the cone opens, its seeds are released.

drought
a time when it does not rain enough to give living things the water they need

evaporate
to heat up and turn from liquid to gas

gas
a kind of matter that changes its size and shape to fill whatever container it is in

germinate
to start to grow from a seed

greenhouse gas
one of the gases in a layer high above Earth, which traps heat in our atmosphere

leaf
the part of a plant where photosynthesis happens

moss
a type of small, nonflowering green plant that does not have proper roots

nectar
a sugary liquid produced by flowers that attracts bees, other insects, birds, and small animals

photosynthesis
how a plant uses water, carbon dioxide, and light to make its own food

pollination
how plants start the process of reproduction

reproduce
to create new life (for example, when plants release seeds and the seeds grow into a new plant)

soil
soft ground in which plants can grow

structure
something containing many parts that are put together

Books to read

Outdoor Science: Habitats by Sonya Newland (Wayland, 2022) shows you how to explore your own habitat. Creepy-crawly safaris, pond explorations, rock-pool adventures, and more all feature in this thoroughly useful, hands-on outdoor learning guide.

Science in Infographics: Habitats by John Richards and Ed Simkins (Wayland, 2021). If you like statistics, numbers, charts, and graphs – if you're fascinated by facts, basically – this is a great way to learn more about the world's habitats.

Body Bits: Eye-Popping Plant Parts and *Body Bits: Astounding Animal Body Facts* written by Paul Mason, illustrations by Dave Smith (Wayland, 2021). Leaning toward the horrifying and humorous, these books feature fascinating facts and funny cartoons, which explain some of the amazing ways that plants and animals have adapted to their habitats.

Darwin's Tree of Life, written by Michael Bright and illustrated by Margaux Carpentier (Wayland, 2020) shows how the incredible range of different plants and animals on Earth developed. This is a beautiful book with plenty of fun facts: want to know why crabs run sideways, or why humans' brains are in their heads, not their feet? This is the place to find the answers.

Places to visit

American Museum of Natural History

200 Central Park West
New York, NY 10024

This museum has displays about all kinds of living things, their life cycles, and their habitats. Don't miss the life-size model of a blue whale in the marine exhibit or the huge skeleton of a *T. Rex* in the dinosaur hall.

Smithsonian National Museum of Natural History

10th St. and Constitution Ave NW
Washington, D.C. 20560

This museum offers hand-on experiences to teach people about the natural world.

Answers

Page 9

A: Yes, roots do hold plants in place.

B: Dizzy was nearly wrong: plants do communicate with each other, they use chemicals to send messages. But plants cannot talk like us, so Dizzy did actually get this sort of right.

C: Yes, most plants do pull in nutrients through their roots.

D: Yes, roots are one of the main places plants store food for later.

Page 13

The monsters got every single answer correct. Fruit (such as apples), corn (which is also a fruit), flowers, and roots (such as carrots) all need energy to help them grow.

Plants also need energy to grow bigger, taller stems and new leaves.

Page 25

1 is a) – of course! Roots are underground, so they could not help plants get sunlight.

2 is also a), because water is one of the three things plants need to make food (the others are light and carbon dioxide).